Birds

Sally Morgan

www.raintreepublishers.co.uk

Visit our website to find out more information about **Raintree** books.

To order:
- ☎ Phone 44 (0) 1865 888113
- 📄 Send a fax to 44 (0) 1865 314091
- 💻 Visit the Raintree Bookshop at **www.raintreepublishers.co.uk** to browse our catalogue and order online.

Produced for Raintree by
White-Thomson Publishing Ltd
Bridgewater Business Centre, 210 High Street,
Lewes, East Sussex, BN7 2NH

First published in Great Britain by Raintree,
Halley Court, Jordan Hill, Oxford OX2 8EJ,
part of Harcourt Education.
Raintree is a registered trademark of Harcourt Education Ltd.

Consultant: Dr Rod Preston-Mafham
Editorial: Katie Orchard, Nick Hunter and Catherine Clarke
Design: Tim Mayer
Picture Research: Morgan Interactive Ltd
Production: Amanda Meaden

Originated by Dot Gradations Ltd
Printed in China by WKT Company Limited

ISBN 1 844 43771 X
09 08 07 06 05
10 9 8 7 6 5 4 3 2 1

British Library Cataloguing in Publication Data
Morgan, Sally
Birds. – (Animal Kingdom)
598
A full catalogue record for this book is available from
the British Library

Acknowledgements
The publishers would like to thank the following for permission
to reproduce photographs: Corbis **Contents**, pp. **8**, **18**, **33**
bottom, **36**, **58**; Digital Vision **Title**, pp. **12**, **21** top, **32**, **41** top,
60 top, **64**; Ecoscene pp. **5** top (Frank Blackburn), **9** top (Peter
Cairns), **10** (Wayne Lawler), **13** top (Phillip Colla), **13** bottom
(Michael Gore), **16** (Sally Morgan), **16-17** (Michael Gore), **21**
bottom (John Farmar), **23** top, **24**, **25**, **29** bottom, **31** (Fritz
Pölking), **34** (Peter Cairns), **35** top (Sally Morgan), **35** bottom
(Michael Gore), **37** top, **39** bottom (Wayne Lawler), **42** (Fritz
Pölking), **43** bottom (Michael Gore), **45** bottom, **47** bottom
(Frank Blackburn), **54-55** (Sally Morgan), **55** top (Ian Beames),
55 bottom (Colin Conway), **56** (Tom Ennis), **57** top (Fritz
Pölking), **60**, **61** (Sally Morgan); Ecoscene-Papilio pp. **7** middle
(Robert Pickett), **14** (Tony Wilson-Bligh), **27** top (Jack
Milchanowski), **38** (Michael Maconachie), **39** top (Brian Cushing),
53 (Jack Milchanowski); Nature Photo Library pp. **30** (Lynn
Stone), **48** right (Peter Cairns); NHPA pp. **6-7**, **7** top (Laurie
Campbell), **9** bottom (Andy Rouse), **11** top (Stephen Dalton), **15**
bottom (Laurie Campbell), **17** inset (Alberto Nardi), **19** top (John
Shaw), **20** (Martin Wendler), **22** (Jonathan and Angela Scott), **26**
(T. Kitchen and V. Hurst), **28** (Andy Rouse), **29** top (Eero
Murtomaki), **33** top (T. Kitchen and V. Hurst), **37** bottom (Ernie
Janes), **40** (Silvestris), **41** bottom (Nigel Dennis), **43** top (Laurie
Campbell), **44** (Manfred Daneggar), **45** top (Stephen Krasemann),
46 (Ann and Steve Toon), **48** left (Mike Lane), **49** (John
Buckingham), **50** (Rod Planck), **51** top (Kevin Schafer), **51**
bottom (Julie Meech), **52** left (Eric Soder), **57** bottom (Daniel
Heuclin); Photodisc pp. **4**, **5** bottom, **11** bottom, **15** top, **19**
bottom, **23** bottom, **27** bottom, **47** top, **52** right, **59**, **62**.

Front cover photograph of gannets is reproduced with
permission of Nature Photo Library (George McCarthy);
back cover photograph of a puffin reproduced with
permission of Corbis.

Every effort has been made to contact copyright holders of any
material reproduced in this book. Any omissions will be rectified
in subsequent printings if notice is given to the publishers.

The paper used to print this book comes from sustainable
resources.

Contents

Any words appearing in the text in bold, **like this**, are explained in the Glossary.

Introducing birds

Birds are one of the few groups of animals that can fly. There are about 9600 different **species** of birds. They range in size from the tiny bee hummingbird, which is just a few centimetres long, to the wandering albatross, which has a wingspan of almost 4 metres. They are found all around the world, from the poles to the **tropics**.

Vertebrates

Birds belong to a large group of animals called **vertebrates**. These are animals with backbones. The backbone is made up of small bones hinged together, with a bundle of nerves (the spinal cord) running through the middle. Other vertebrates include fish, amphibians, **reptiles** and **mammals**.

Classification key

KINGDOM	Animalia
PHYLUM	Chordata
SUB-PHYLUM	Vertebrata
CLASS	**Aves**
ORDERS	29
FAMILIES	180
SPECIES	9600

Bird features

Birds are **adapted** to flight. Their fore limbs are modified to form wings and they have lightweight bones. Their collar bones are joined together to form a 'wishbone'. All birds are covered in feathers. Feathers are unique to the birds and without them birds could not fly. Birds have a beak, which is formed from their jaws, but they lack teeth. They have a third eyelid called a **nictitating membrane** that is tough and transparent. It cleans the surface of the eye by moving from side to side. All birds are **endothermic** or 'warm-blooded' (see pages 14–15).

◄ The ability of birds to fly has allowed them to spread throughout the world.

4

Egg layers

Like most fish, amphibians and reptiles, birds lay eggs. However, unlike the eggs of other animals, birds' eggs have hard, protective shells. Most birds take great care of their eggs, laying them in a nest. The eggs are kept warm, or **incubated**, by one of the parent birds until they hatch. They care for their chicks until they are old enough to fend for themselves.

▲ Many birds build a nest in which to lay their eggs and raise their young.

Classification

Living organisms are classified, or organized, according to how closely related one **organism** is to another. The basic group in classification is the species, for example, humans belong to the species *Homo sapiens*. A species is a group of individuals that are similar to each other and that can **interbreed** with one another. Species are grouped together into genera (singular: genus). A genus may contain a number of species that share some features. *Homo* is the human genus. Genera are grouped together in families, the families grouped into orders and the orders grouped into classes. Aves is the class of birds. Classes are grouped together in phyla (singular: phylum) and finally the phyla are grouped into kingdoms. Kingdoms are the largest groups. Birds belong to the animal kingdom. (To find out more see pages 58–59.)

beak adapted to the bird's method of feeding

wing

▶ All birds have two wings, two legs and a body that is covered in feathers.

body covered in feathers

leg that ends in toes

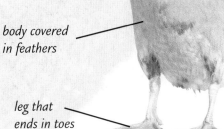

5

Bird life cycles and behaviour

The life cycle of the bird starts with the egg. Bird eggs vary in size, colour and number. A bird's egg is protected by a hard shell. The shell allows oxygen to pass into the egg. Inside the shell there is an **embryo**, which grows into the young bird. The embryo floats on the surface of the yellow yolk, which supplies it with the nourishment it needs. Around the yolk is the egg white, or **albumen**. This supports and protects the embryo.

Nest building

Most birds build nests from moss, lichen, twigs and leaves. Some birds use other nesting materials including animal hair, other birds' feathers and even artificial materials, such as plastic and wool. The nest is usually lined with feathers pulled from the female's chest. The most common form of nest is cup-shaped, but some birds build nests with entrances underneath. Most birds build their nests in a place where it will be safe from **predators**, such as high in a tree or in the middle of a hedge, but others build their nests on the ground. A few birds do not build a nest at all, simply laying their eggs on the ground or in holes.

▼ Mute swans build a large nest, up to 1 metre wide, in which they lay up to 8 eggs.

Incubation

After **mating**, the female bird lays an egg every one or two days. When the batch of eggs, or **clutch**, is complete, one of the parent birds sits on the eggs to keep them warm. This is called **incubation**. The period of incubation varies from one **species** to another.

▲ Mute swans care for their young, called cygnets, for at least five months.

▲ This duckling is about to hatch. It fills the egg and all of the yolk has been used. It breaks out of the shell using its special **egg tooth**.

Amazing facts

- The ostrich lays the world's largest egg at 1.5 kilograms.
- Not all birds incubate their eggs themselves. For example, megapodes (large game birds from Australia and New Guinea) incubate their eggs in the ground, piling earth and rotting vegetation over them to form a mound.

Young chicks

Most chicks are blind and featherless and completely helpless when they hatch. These are called **nidicolous** chicks. They depend on their parents to look after them and keep them warm. These chicks remain in the nest for a relatively long time. In contrast, young waterfowl, such as geese and ducks, and game birds, such as pheasants, are born with their eyes open and with a covering of downy feathers. They are able to run around within minutes of hatching. Usually they follow the parents around, but are able to feed themselves. These are **nidifugous** young.

Young birds are said to **fledge** when they leave the nest. Some do not fledge until they have grown some flight feathers and they can fly away. Others will fledge while they still have downy feathers.

Attracting a mate

Most birds rely on brightly coloured **plumage**, songs and dance displays to attract a **mate**. Often the female is attracted to the male with the most colourful feathers, the loudest call or the most impressive dance.

Plumage

Female birds tend to have drab brown feathers. This colour blends well with their surroundings and it means that the female is less visible while she is nesting. The male, in contrast, may have brightly coloured feathers to attract the attention of a female. For example, the male peacock has an amazing train of long tail feathers. When he displays in front of the female, he raises his tail feathers to form a fan behind his head. The female peacocks usually choose the male with the largest fan.

Some birds lose their bright plumage after **breeding**. The tufted puffin (*Fratercola cirrhata*), for example, has a clown-like white face, colourful red beak and long, yellow tufts of feathers. After the breeding season, the beak becomes less colourful, the tufts are lost and the white face turns dark grey.

▲ Many male birds, such as this beautiful peacock, are more colourful than the females, especially during the breeding season.

Song and dance

Many male birds sing to attract a mate. Often an older male bird with a better selection of songs is more successful at attracting a mate than a younger male. Other birds attract the female by displaying, or dancing. Some sing and dance.

Male black grouse (*Tetrao tetrix*) gather together in areas called leks, where they traditionally display. The males strut in front of each other, with the head pointing up and the tail feathers fanned out, while the females watch from nearby trees. They make a noisy 'rookooing' song that can carry up to 3 kilometres. Many male birds of paradise have wonderful feathers. However, brightly coloured feathers alone are not enough to impress female birds of paradise, so the males perform gymnastic displays as well! They hang upside down on a branch, shake their feathers and even bounce up and down.

▲ Male black grouse gather at display grounds called leks to compete for mates. Each male struts around and fans his feathers to attract a female.

Amazing facts

- Courtship in the Japanese crane (*Grus japonensis*) involves dancing. Groups of cranes gather together and begin to bow and leap in front of one another. They flap their wings, jump in the air and run around.

- During the courtship of the greater bird of paradise, as many as 20 males gather together in a tree to dance. The female selects the most impressive.

- As a male peacock gets older, his feathers get longer, so the oldest birds have the largest fans. They are more attractive to the female, having survived for longer.

◄ Japanese cranes take part in a complex dance with the birds bowing or bobbing in front of each other.

9

Feathery bodies

Everything about the bird is **adapted** for flight, from the shape and weight of the **skeleton** to the arrangement of the limb bones and the covering of feathers.

Skeleton

The bird's skeleton is very different from that of a **mammal**. Birds have four limbs, but the front limbs, or 'arms', have been modified to form wings. Birds have fewer bones in the arm, especially in the wrist and hand, which makes it more rigid and prevents the wing from bending in the middle. The breastbone has a deep extension, which sticks out to form a **keel** and provides a large area for the attachment of flight muscles.

Most of the bones of the bird are hollow and lightweight, allowing the bird to get off the ground easily. Although the bones are light, they are also strong, with struts across the hollow centres. However, diving birds, such as ducks and penguins, have more solid bones, which makes them heavier in the water and less **buoyant**. This helps them to dive. The heaviest birds, the ostriches, are flightless.

Birds have 11–25 neck bones, or vertebrae. This makes the neck very flexible and allows the bird to reach all parts of the body for **preening**.

◄ Preening keeps this crane's feathers in top condition.

◀ Among the aerial acrobats of the bird world are the swallows with their short broad wings and forked tail. This swallow is taking a drink while flying.

Amazing facts

- The sword-billed hummingbird has a beak that is longer than its body, so it has to preen itself using one foot, while balancing on the other foot.
- Ducks moult their feathers over a three-week period. During this time they are flightless and they have to take to the water to escape **predators**.

Feathery covering

Feathers grow from the skin and are made of keratin, the same material that forms hair in mammals. Feathers are formed of a central shaft (quill) to which branches, or **barbs**, are attached. The barbs are held together by tiny hooks. The largest feathers are the flight feathers, found on the wing and tail. They are rigid and provide lift (see page 12) for flight. Contour feathers are smaller and softer. They form a smooth covering over the body. Beneath the contour feathers is a layer of down – small, fluffy feathers that lie next to the skin, forming an **insulating** layer to keep the bird warm.

Birds spend much time each day preening – carefully cleaning and arranging the feathers with their beak. They have a special gland near the base of their tail that secretes an oil, which they use to keep their feathers in good condition. This is particularly important in water birds that need to waterproof their feathers. Each year birds lose their feathers, or **moult**, although not always all their feathers at the same time. New ones grow in their place.

▶ A flight feather is stiff and unevenly shaped, with a long quill.

11

Bird flight

In order to rise up into the air, and then to stay in the air and move forwards, a bird needs to generate 'lift'. A bird's wing is shaped so that the upper surface is curved outwards. As a bird moves forward, air flows over the surfaces of the wings. Air has to move a slightly longer distance and at a slightly faster speed over the upper surface of the wing than the lower surface. This causes a difference in pressure, creating an upward force called lift.

Flapping and gliding

There are two main forms of flight – flapping and gliding. In flapping flight, the bird moves its wings up and down. On the upstroke, the bird bends its wings so that the tips come close to the body and then raises and extends its wings so that they are at full stretch. During the down stroke the bird brings its wings down and this generates the power that moves the bird forwards. Most birds flap their wings to get airborne.

In gliding flight the bird holds out its wings to catch wind or air currents. This saves energy because the bird hardly moves its wings. Warm air rises. Gliding birds rise up into the air on warm air currents, called **thermals**, and then gradually spiral down again before finding another rising thermal.

The hummingbird neither flaps up and down nor glides in order to hover. Its wings can move backwards and forwards in a figure of eight. Hummingbirds are incredibly manoeuvrable, darting backwards and forwards. They are the only birds that can fly backwards.

▼ These sandhill cranes have long, broad wings, which are well suited to flying long distances.

▲ Brown boobies make use of gliding flight as they scan the sea for shoals of fish.

Amazing facts

- The albatross may glide for several hours without beating its wings.
- When diving down towards its **prey**, the peregrine falcon can reach speeds of 320 kilometres (200 miles) per hour or more.
- The tiny bee hummingbird (*Calypte helenae*) has to beat its wings 200 times a second in order to produce enough lift to stay airborne.

▼ This hummingbird is hovering as it inserts its beak deep into a flower to sip the nectar with its long tongue.

Wing shape

Wings come in different shapes, each **adapted** to a particular type of flight. For example, gliding birds have long, broad wings, while fast-flying birds, such as swifts, swallows and falcons, have swept-back curved wings with pointed tips. Birds, such as pheasants, that need a fast take off in order to escape from a **predator**, have broad, rounded wings.

13

Keeping warm

Birds are **endothermic**, which means they have a relatively constant body temperature, regardless of the surrounding temperature. Their body temperature is about 40° Celsius. This means that they have to eat enough food to provide energy to keep their body warm.

Insulation

Feathers have a vital role to play in keeping a bird warm, especially the down feathers that **insulate** the body against heat loss (see page 11). In cold weather many birds puff up their feathers. This creates lots of air spaces, which trap heat. Some birds, such as snowy owls (*Nyctea scandiaca*) and grouse, have feathers right down to their toes, which reduces heat loss from their legs. Another way of staying warm is to shiver. Shivering is caused by muscles contracting and this generates heat. Most birds living in cold climates shiver constantly at night. This keeps them from freezing during the long, dark hours when they are not moving.

Becoming torpid

Some birds live in climates where the temperature falls dramatically at night. For example, chickadees of the northern forests of North America and hummingbirds living at high altitude experience this. Hummingbirds and chickadees get around the problem by becoming **torpid** – where their internal temperature falls to well below normal and they become inactive. This way they do not use valuable energy reserves trying to keep warm. They become active again when the sun rises and the temperatures get warmer. Some birds can remain in a state of torpor for weeks until conditions become more favourable.

◀ Small birds lose a lot of heat in cold weather. This robin has fluffed up its feathers to trap air between them in order to stay warm.

Surviving the cold

Penguins are an example of a bird that lives in a cold climate. They have a thick layer of fat, called **blubber**, beneath their skin to insulate their body and stop heat from escaping. To avoid losing valuable heat through their feet, they have an unusual arrangement of blood vessels called a **heat exchanger**. Blood vessels carrying warm blood from the body flow very close to the blood vessels carrying cold blood from the feet. The cold blood gets warmed up by the warm blood. By the time the blood from the body has reached the feet it has given all its heat to the blood returning to the body. This way very little heat is lost to the environment.

Amazing facts

- The eider duck has a thick layer of downy feathers on its breast, which it plucks off to insulate its nest against the extreme cold of the Arctic. 'Eiderdown' quilts were once filled with feathers from this duck.

- Becoming torpid overnight can save a bird 20 per cent of the energy it would have used shivering.

▲ The snowy owl's feathers extend over its toes and along its beak to provide maximum insulation.

◀ Waterfowl, such as this eider duck, have a thick layer of downy feathers to insulate their body against the cold.

Migration

Many birds **migrate** to escape cold winters or hot summers, or to find suitable **breeding** grounds and food sources. Some birds move annually between summer breeding grounds and overwintering sites, usually returning to the same areas each year. For example, during the short summer in the Arctic, food is plentiful. Thousands of swans, ducks and geese flock to the Arctic to feed and breed. However, the temperatures fall well below freezing during the long, harsh winter, and food becomes scarce. The birds that spend the summer in the Arctic migrate south to winter feeding grounds where they can find food. When the time to migrate approaches, birds gather together so that they can travel in large flocks. Since the Arctic summer is short, birds have to breed quickly so their chicks have as long as possible to grow before they fly south. Any chicks that hatch late may not be ready to fly with the adults.

Preparing for migration

Migration can be risky. The distances can be long and the birds have to be fit enough to fly. They prepare for the journey by laying down fat, which they will use to fuel their bodies on their journey. Many birds die on the migration. They may starve, be blown off course by bad weather or be killed by **predators.**

▼ These whooper swans have flown thousands of kilometres from Siberia to the UK where they spend the winter.

▲ The Arctic tern breeds in the Arctic and overwinters in the Antarctic. It spends much of the year in flight over the world's oceans.

▲ Migrating waterfowl, such as these snow geese, often fly in a 'V' formation. By flying just behind the lead bird, in its slip stream, the rest of the flock use up less energy.

Navigating

Birds can fly thousands of kilometres and end up at exactly the same place, year after year. They make use of several different clues to find their way. As they fly south, they can detect the change in day length. They also use the Sun, the Moon and stars for guidance.

Birds may be able to detect changes in Earth's magnetic field (a bit like an internal compass). Also, they may look for landmarks, which they observed on previous journeys, although young birds have been known to migrate safely on their own for the first time. City lights can interfere with a bird's sense of direction.

Amazing facts

- The tiny ruby-throated hummingbird (*Archiolochus colubris*) migrates 1000 kilometres (620 miles) across the water of the Gulf of Mexico, a journey that takes 20 hours, without rest.

- The wandering albatross (*Diomedes exulans*) circles the Southern Ocean for two years without landing before returning to its nesting grounds on islands.

- Each year the Arctic tern (*Sterna paradisaea*) travels from the Arctic to the Antarctic and back again, a round trip of about 40,000 kilometres (25,000 miles).

17

Bird orders

There are about 9600 **species** of birds, divided into 29 orders. The different orders have slightly different **skeletons**, each **adapted** to a particular way of life. The position and length of the legs, the number of toes or the shape of the wing may vary. For example, waterfowl have short legs with webbed feet for swimming. Flamingos and stilts have long legs for wading in shallow water, while woodpeckers have legs that are adapted to climbing trees.

Digesting food

Birds do not have teeth, so birds that eat seeds and other hard foods have a **gizzard** (a pouch full of grit) in which food is ground up. Birds swallow grit to aid this process. Some birds have a **crop** – a pouch off the oesophagus (the tube that runs from the mouth to the stomach) in which food can be stored. This allows the bird to feed in a hurry and digest the food later. Game birds, hawks, owls and waterfowl have gizzards and crops.

Classification key

KINGDOM	Animalia
PHYLUM	Chordata
SUB-PHYLUM	Vertebrata
CLASS	**Aves**
ORDERS	29
FAMILIES	180
SPECIES	9600

▼ Great egrets have a long neck, legs and beak. They do not have a crop.

Evolution

Birds **evolved** from **reptiles**. Imagine millions of years ago a reptile leaping off rocks or trees in an attempt to escape **predators**. It would spread its limbs and try to glide using its scales to slow down its descent. In time the scales became lighter and elongated and became feathers. Birds and reptiles still share many similarities such as bone structure, the arrangement of muscle and joints, and egg-laying. However, reptiles have scales while birds have feathers. Birds also have wings.

The earliest complete skeleton of a bird dates back 150 million years. It is called *Archaeopteryx* and it resembled a small dinosaur with a lizard-like tail, a mouth full of small teeth and wings with feathers. This early bird evolved to lose its tail and teeth, and many of its bones joined together to make a rigid skeleton, while the neck got longer. About 80 million years ago the **ancestors** of birds such as hawks, herons, ducks and owls appeared, followed by songbirds.

▲ The spoonbill sweeps its spoon-shaped beak through the water from side to side to create currents. The currents dislodge small animals that the bird eats.

Amazing facts

- The smallest bird is the bee hummingbird. It weighs just a couple of grams and is about 5 centimetres in length.

- The **nictitating membrane** (see page 4) of diving birds has a built-in contact lens to improve vision underwater.

- The largest bird that has ever existed was the moa, a flightless bird, which weighed a massive 227 kilograms. This **extinct** bird looked like a giant ostrich.

► The Harris hawk has a strong, hooked beak and excellent eyesight to spot prey on the ground.

Flightless birds

Most birds can fly, but a few birds are flightless. These are the ratites, tinamous and penguins. Ratites are birds such as ostriches, rheas, cassowaries and kiwis. The flightless birds make up six orders – ostriches (Struthioniformes), rheas (Rheiformes), cassowaries (Casuariiformes), kiwis (Apterygiformes), tinamous (Tinamiformes) and penguins (Sphenisciformes). Penguins are described in more detail on pages 22–25.

A lost skill

Flightless birds have **evolved** from birds that could once fly. Ratites have a flat breastbone, which lacks a **keel** for the attachment of flight muscles. Large, flightless birds such as the emu, cassowary, rhea and ostrich have long legs and necks. The ratites range in size from kiwis at 50 centimetres to the ostrich, which reaches heights of 2.75 metres. Ratites have evolved to lose at least one toe (ostriches have only two toes). Their long legs give them a long stride, which means they can cover the ground with ease. They have wings, but they are small. Their **nidifugous** chicks (see page 7) are born with downy feathers.

Classification key	
CLASS	Aves
ORDERS	**6 (Apterygiformes, Casuariiformes, Rheiformes, Sphenisciformes Struthioniformes and Tinamiformes)**
FAMILIES	7
SPECIES	74

▼ Rheas are found in South America. They have three toes and each of their wings ends in a claw.

▶ The ostrich can reach a height of 2.75 metres and weigh 135 kilograms.

▼ The cassowary has a distinctive helmet on its head, called a casque. The centre of the casque is made of a tough, elastic foam-like substance.

Amazing facts

- The ostrich can run at speeds of up to 70 kilometres (43 miles) per hour for as long as 30 minutes at a time.
- The male emu **incubates** the eggs and cares for the young for up to eight months.

Why flightless?

Scientists know that these birds were once able to fly from looking at their **skeletons**. They have wings, although their wings are reduced in size. Many of their bones are hollow, which is another **adaptation** for flight. It is believed that some of the flightless birds evolved in habitats where they had few **predators** so they did not need to take to the air to escape. Some, such as the kiwi, are found on isolated islands where there were no predators. In other birds it is thought that being large and strong was more important for survival than being able to fly. The ostrich, for example, lives in places where there are large predators such as lions and leopards. The ostrich has long legs and can run very quickly. It can also use them as weapons, to kick an attacker. The tinamou is slightly different to the others. It is a small, secretive bird that looks like a partridge. It can fly for a short distance, but it tends to stay on the ground.

Penguins

Penguins have short legs and wings that look like flippers. Their legs are positioned so far back that they have to stand completely upright while they are on land. This body shape is **streamlined** in water and ideal for swimming. Penguins are found in the Southern Hemisphere, especially in the Antarctic, and the islands of the Southern Ocean. A few are found in South Africa, Australia, South America and as far north as the Galapagos Islands, which lie close to the equator.

Cold adaptations

Most penguins live in the Antarctic where temperatures rarely rise above freezing, all year round. It is amazing that any animal could survive there, but penguins are well **adapted** to this hostile environment. Penguins are covered in a thick layer of feathers and **blubber**, which helps to keep heat within the bird's body. Their feathers are pointed and form layers that overlap each other. The feathers are also well waterproofed. Penguins have a **heat exchanger** in their feet (see page 15), which means that little heat is lost while the birds stand on the ice.

Amazing facts

- Magellanic and Humboldt penguins from the coasts of South America are unusual as they nest in shallow burrows where they are protected from **predators**, such as kelp gulls, and from the hot sun.
- Chinstrap penguins are particularly noisy and are sometimes also called stonecracker penguins because of their piercing voices.

◀ The chinstrap penguin is easily identified by the black line that runs from ear to ear under its chin.

▲ King penguins gather in large colonies. Their chicks have brown fluffy feathers, which are replaced by adult feathers when they are about ten months old.

Getting around

Penguins tend to waddle on land, which can appear awkward, but they are capable of walking considerable distances. They 'toboggan' on their fronts over snow and ice, using their feet and flippers to push forward. Once in the water they are very graceful. Their wings are modified to form stiff, flat flippers for swimming. The bones are flatter than those of other birds and solid to give more strength and weight. The whole of the flipper is rigid. They swim just as if they were flying, by flapping their wings to propel themselves forward. They can dive to the depths to catch fish, each dive lasting up to 20 minutes.

▲ The Humboldt penguin nests along the coasts of Chile and Peru, and feeds on fish and squid.

Living together

Penguins live together in large groups called **colonies**. In some cases the colonies may number hundreds of thousands of birds. The female penguin usually makes a simple nest from pebbles, feathers and sometimes grass. One or two eggs are laid, which are **incubated** by the male. However, some **species** of penguin, such as the emperor penguin, do not make a nest at all.

Classification key	
CLASS	Aves
ORDER	**Sphenisciformes**
FAMILIES	1
SPECIES	17

The emperor penguin

The emperor penguin is one of the few animals that can survive the harsh conditions of Antarctica. In the middle of the dark Antarctic winter, the emperor penguins move from the pack ice around the edge of the continent and walk inland to the place where they will set up their rookery.

Left on the ice

The female lays her single egg and passes it to the male. The female walks back to the sea to feed, leaving the male on the ice. She will be gone two months, returning just as the chick hatches. The male **incubates** the egg alone, with the egg balanced on his feet and covered by a flap of skin. The male penguins huddle together to conserve their body heat. The huddle is constantly on the move, with all the birds shuffling forwards, the birds taking it in turns to be on the colder outside. They do not eat while they are incubating, so they gradually lose weight.

After two months the chick hatches and the male **regurgitates** enough food to give the new-born chick one meal. If all goes to plan, the female returns just as the chick is born and takes over from the male. If the female does not arrive, the male abandons the chick, which dies, and returns to the sea to feed. He cannot wait for the female because he will have lost as much as 40 per cent of his body weight and any delay means that he will be too weak to reach the sea. Over the next five to six months, the chick is fed about fourteen times – seven times by each parent. At first the parents take it in turns to return to the sea. When the chick is older it is left with other chicks in one of several special areas of the rookery while both parents go to sea to feed.

◄ Emperor penguins have to survive the severe Antarctic weather and temperatures well below freezing for much of the year.

Too close or too far?

Emperor penguins have to choose the site of their rookery very carefully. If the rookery is too far from open water it will take the parents too long to make the trip to the sea and back enough times to feed the chick. If this happens the chicks will die. By summer, the ice where the emperors have their rookery breaks up and floats out to sea. If the rookery is placed too close to open water, the ice may break up before the chicks are old enough to survive. Once the ice breaks up the chicks are on their own. If they have not grown their adult feathers they will not be able to go into the water to feed themselves.

Classification key

CLASS	Aves
ORDER	Sphenisciformes
FAMILY	Spheniscidae
GENUS	*Aptenodytes*
SPECIES	***Aptenodytes forsteri***

Amazing facts

- An adult emperor penguin can weigh more than 30 kilograms and reach a height of up to 115 centimetres.

- The average life expectancy of an emperor penguin is 20 years, but a small number have lived to 50 years of age.

◄ Young emperor penguin chicks rely on both parents for food.

Swans, geese and ducks

Swans, geese, ducks and screamers are called waterfowl because they live close to water. Waterfowl are found all around the world. Most are strong swimmers and fliers. Their feet are webbed between the first three toes. This creates a large surface, which can press against the water, like flippers, to propel the bird forwards. Waterfowl have legs that are positioned further back than other birds so that they can use their legs to move themselves forwards through water. Waterfowl tend to be heavier than those birds that spend of a lot of time in the air. Their bones are solid, so that they are heavy enough to dive and swim underwater, although not all of them dive.

Diving and swimming birds have more downy feathers to provide waterproofing and **insulation**. The **preen** gland near the base of their tail produces an oily secretion, which they spread over their feathers. The oil causes water to run off their feathers, making them waterproof.

Because they are relatively heavy birds, waterfowl need to build up speed to become airborne. They tend to 'run' over the surface of the water to generate sufficient force to lift off. They land on water, too, using their webbed feet as brakes when they hit the surface of the water, and skid to a halt.

Classification key

CLASS	Aves
ORDER	**Anseriformes**
FAMILIES	2 – Anhimidae (6 species of screamers and the magpie goose) and Anatidae (153 species of ducks, geese and swans)
SPECIES	159

Amazing facts

- Some waterfowl have been kept by humans for more than 4000 years.
- The merganser not only flies quickly, reaching speeds of up to 100 kilometres (62 miles) per hour, but it also swims rapidly under water to catch fish.

▼ Geese, such as this Canada goose, need a running take-off to get up into the air. They run across the surface of the water to gain lift and speed.

▶ During the **breeding** season, the male wood duck is far more colourful than the female duck.

Feeding

Most waterfowl have flat, shovel-shaped beaks. This shape is perfect for extracting food from mud and water. They feed on a variety of foods including plants, **aquatic** insects, clams and other **invertebrate** animals. Screamers, however, have a chicken-like beak, which is better suited to eating insects.

Breeding

Most waterfowl build large nests on the ground. Some choose to nest on islands in ponds to be safe from **predators** such as foxes. A few ducks, such as wood ducks and mergansers, nest in hollows in tree trunks. Their nests are built from grass and reeds. Waterfowl young are **nidifugous**. Within minutes of hatching the young are up and running around. They can feed on their own, too. The young follow their parents to water and can swim within hours. Young waterfowl are born with an instinct to recognize their parents. This behaviour is called imprinting and it means that the young stay near to a parent and follow them everywhere.

▲ The mallard is the world's most common **species** of duck and is found near water in towns and countryside.

27

Birds of prey

Birds of **prey**, or **raptors**, are skilled **predators** equipped with sharp claws and hooked beaks. They are found around the world, from the high mountains to the rainforests.

Catching prey

Birds of prey have incredible eyesight. During the day a bird of prey can see at least two-and-a-half times further than a human, and possibly as much as eight times further. This makes it easy for them to spot prey from a distance.

Most birds of prey feed on live animals such as rabbits, mice, **reptiles** and other birds. Although they have a sharp beak, birds of prey kill with their feet. The larger birds of prey, such as fish eagles, bald eagles and ospreys, swoop down to grab fish from the water. Smaller birds of prey, such as the peregrine falcon, snatch prey in mid-air. The birds dive at speed towards their prey, grabbing it with their claws. Their needle-like claws pierce the body of their prey, damaging the vital organs and snapping the backbone.

Once they have caught their prey, birds of prey usually return to a perch to feed. Eagles have a **crop** where they can store food when their stomach is full. The crop also separates feathers, fur and scales from meat. After the meal, the eagle **regurgitates** the indigestible feathers, fur or scales from the **gizzard** as a pellet.

◀ The osprey is a powerful predator that can catch and lift large salmon from the water.

Scavengers

Vultures and many kites feed on **carrion** (dead animals). They spend hours gliding on currents of warm air, looking for food. Their excellent eyesight allows them to spot a meal on the ground from a great height. They also have a good sense of smell. Vultures gather around the dead body and squabble over the remains. Griffon vultures have a long neck with no contour feathers. This allows the birds to reach deep into the bodies of dead animals without their feathers becoming covered in blood. Unlike the other birds of prey, vultures have broad, chicken-like feet, with weak talons, which are not suitable for grasping.

▲ Most birds of prey, such as this sea eagle, have powerful, curved talons, which they use to kill their prey.

Amazing facts

○ Peregrine falcons dive at speeds in excess of 320 kilometres (200 miles) per hour and strike their prey with such force that the impact produces clouds of feathers.

○ The Andean condor has the largest wingspan of any land bird. It glides above the Andes mountains at heights of up to 5500 metres looking for carrion.

○ The golden eagle builds its nests, called eyries, on the ledges of cliffs and in tall trees. The nest, built from twigs and branches, may be up to 2 metres across.

Classification key

CLASS	Aves
ORDER	**Falconiformes**
FAMILIES	3
SPECIES	approximately 300

► Vultures, such as this Ruppell's griffon vulture, gather around carcasses and quickly strip all the meat from the bones.

The bald eagle

The bald eagle (*Haliaeetus leucocephalus*) is one of the largest birds of **prey**. It lives only in North America where it is found from Alaska to Mexico. The eagle is not really bald, but the head is covered in white feathers.

Bald eagles living along the coast and on major lakes and rivers feed mainly on fish, especially salmon. Even though they are fish eaters, bald eagles will take whatever prey is available. Sometimes bald eagles will feed on **carrion**. The carcass of a seal, for example, is a large food supply. Rich in fat and protein, a seal's body will feed a group of eagles for days.

Catching a meal

Once an eagle spots a fish swimming or floating near the surface of the water, it glides down and snatches the fish out of the water with a quick swipe of its claws.

Amazing facts

- Bald eagles were shot by farmers as they were thought to prey on livestock. In 1940 the Bald and Golden Eagle Protection Act was passed. Although numbers have increased, the bald eagle is still classed as a threatened species in the USA.
- Salmon return to rivers to spawn and die. The vast number of dead bodies attracts many animals, including large numbers of bald eagles.

▼ Pairs of bald eagles build huge nests in trees or on the ground. The female lays two to three eggs.

Classification key

CLASS	Aves
ORDER	Falconiformes
FAMILY	Accipitridae
GENUS	*Haliaeetus*
SPECIES	***Haliaeetus leucocephalus***

Eagles have a special locking mechanism for their claws. When the open claws hit the prey, they instantly close and cannot be opened again until the eagle lands on a solid surface. Bald eagles can lift about 2 kilograms, so they can carry a salmon or other small **mammals**. The eagle returns to its perch where it holds its prey with one claw and holds on to its perch with the other. It tears off large chunks of flesh with its beak.

Bald eagles do not have to eat every day. Hunting uses up a lot of energy, so between hunts the eagle has to rest. It is estimated that only one out of every eighteen attacks is successful. But if the bird goes too long without food, it may not be able to hunt effectively in order to survive. Each eagle hunts in a given area, its **territory**, which varies in size depending on the availability of food. In areas where food is plentiful bald eagles have a smaller territory.

▲ The bald eagle swoops down at great speed and snatches fish lying near the surface of the water.

▶ An adult bald eagle has a wingspan of about 2.5 metres.

Stealing food

The bald eagle may steal food from other birds of prey, especially smaller eagle **species**. First, it chases the other bird to make the bird drop its kill. If this does not work, the bald eagle will attack the smaller bird.

31

Owls

Owls are **predatory** birds. They are similar in many ways to the birds of **prey** with their hooked beaks and sharp claws. Some biologists think they should be classified with the birds of prey. Many owls hunt at night, relying on their excellent sense of hearing to find their prey.

▲ The great horned owl has large, horn-like ear tufts. It is a North American owl.

Owls have well-developed senses. Like other predatory birds they have large eyes, especially the owls that hunt by day. Owls also have exceptional hearing. A barn owl can hear a mouse moving on the ground in the dark, while a great horned owl can hear a snake slithering through the grass. Each ear has a long, vertical opening, which allows more sound to pass to the inner ear inside the skull. Owls also have one ear set slightly higher than the other, enabling them to identify the exact origin of a sound. The feathers around the ear and face are shaped to funnel the sound into the ear.

Silent flight

Most birds make quite a lot of noise as they fly, but the owl flies silently. Owls' wings have feathers with soft leading edges, which allow the air to flow through them absolutely silently.

Classification key	
CLASS	Aves
ORDER	**Strigiformes**
FAMILIES	2
SPECIES	more than 130

Down in one!

Owls swallow their food whole because they have no **crop**. This means that the bird swallows the indigestible bits, such as bones, feathers, beaks and hair, as well as meat. Once inside the stomach the indigestible parts are separated and then **regurgitated** as a small pellet.

Mixed ages

Owls nest in cavities in trees, among rocks and, in the case of barn owls, in farm buildings. Often they simply lay their eggs in the cavity without any lining material. Owls lay between two and seven eggs. Unlike most other birds, the chicks do not all hatch at about the same time. Instead, they hatch at two-day intervals, which means that the owls raise chicks that differ in age. The first chicks to hatch are the most likely to survive. If food becomes scarce, the younger chicks die.

▼ Most owls feed on small **mammals**, birds or insects.

Amazing facts

- The great grey owl (*Strix nebulosa*) can hear a field vole running under half a metre of snow and then dive through the snow to catch it.
- Owls' eyes are fixed in their sockets. Owls have to turn their heads to shift their gaze. They have extra neck bones so they can turn their head three-quarters of the way around.

▼ Most owls hunt at night. The soft edges of their wing feathers muffle the sound of their flight.

Game birds

Game birds include grouse, partridges, pheasants and peacocks, all birds that were once hunted for food. Today, many game birds, such as turkeys, chickens, peafowl and guineafowl are raised on farms rather than being hunted.

Game birds are mostly ground-dwelling birds. Most have a plump body with short legs. They have broad and heavy feet, with a hind toe, which are well **adapted** to running and scratching the ground. The beak is short, stout and often down-curved. They have short, rounded wings with stiff, slightly bent wing feathers. These wings are poorly adapted for sustained flight. Game birds usually fly only short distances, for example, to escape a **predator**.

Feeding and life cycle

Game birds scratch the ground with their feet to find food. They generally feed on plant material, such as seeds, leaves, fruit and buds, as well as insects and other small **invertebrates** such as snails and slugs.

Game birds live together in small groups called coveys. Most nest on the ground, where their nests blend in with their surroundings. They usually lay a large **clutch** of eggs. The chicks are born with downy feathers and they are **nidifugous**, as they can feed themselves within a few hours of hatching.

◄ The red grouse is found on moorland. Females lay up to ten eggs on the ground. The young follow the female all summer.

► A male turkey courts females by fanning his tail feathers, spreading his wings and making a gobbling sound.

The Australian mallee fowl lay their eggs in a huge heap of leaves and twigs. As the plant material rots, it releases heat and this keeps the eggs warm. The **incubation** period is about eleven weeks, during which time the male keeps a close watch on the heap, removing material if it gets too hot and adding more if it cools down.

Classification key

CLASS	Aves
ORDER	**Galliformes**
FAMILIES	4
SPECIES	about 260

Amazing facts

○ Turkeys were hunted in the wild and farmed in parts of the Americas before 1492 and were then brought to Europe.

○ Ptarmigans live in upland areas and change colour during the year to blend with their habitat. In summer they are dark brown and white, but in winter they turn all white.

○ The helmeted guinea fowl reacts to danger with a piercing alarm call that sounds like the screeching of broken machinery.

Male and female differences

The males and females of some **species** of game bird look very different, the male having brightly coloured **plumage** whereas the female is a drab brown. The male ring-necked pheasant (*Phasianus colchicus*), for example, has copper-coloured feathers, a shiny green-purple neck and a patch of bright red around the eyes, while the females are brown all over.

◄ This vulturine guinea fowl is found on the grasslands of central and southern Africa, where it lives in flocks.

Shorebirds, gulls and auks

The Charadriiformes is a very varied order including the waders, gulls and auks. These birds are found on coasts, lakes, marshes and meadows. A few are found in thick woodland and in deserts. They tend to have slender legs and beaks, which are **adapted** to their diet.

Three sub-orders

This order is usually divided into three sub-orders. The waders (Charadrii) are typical shorebirds, most of which feed by probing in the mud or picking food off the surface in coastal and wetland habitats. Gulls and their relatives (Lari) have webbed feet and a salt gland above the eye. These are generally larger birds, which take fish from the sea. Some gulls and skuas will take food from beaches, or rob smaller birds. A few have become adapted to life inland and are found in cities, towns and on farmland. Auks (Alcidae) are coastal birds, which nest on sea cliffs and dive under water to catch fish. Auks are stocky, marine birds with webbed feet, no hind toe and an upright stance, for example, guillemots.

Classification key

CLASS	Aves
ORDER	**Charadriiformes**
SUB-ORDERS	3 – Charadrii (waders), Lari (gulls) and Alcidae (auks)
FAMILIES	16
SPECIES	350

▼ Puffins spend the winter at sea and then come ashore to nest in summer. Their large beak is most colourful during the **breeding** season.

Beak design

A bird's beak may seem to be hard and lacking in feeling, but it contains many nerve endings at the end, making it incredibly sensitive. A wading bird pushing its beak into the mud can feel the presence of a **prey** animal and distinguish it from a stone or a piece of seaweed. The avocet has a graceful, needle-like beak that curves upwards towards the end. It sweeps its beak through the water just above the mud in search of insects. Turnstones flip over pebbles on the beach to reveal small animals hiding beneath. Oystercatchers may use their beak to hammer open the tough shells of mussels and cockles or act like pincers to pull worms out of the sand.

Long legs

Many waders have long legs with a joint that makes the leg appear to bend backwards. Although this joint looks as if it is the knee, it is in fact the bird's ankle. The lower leg below this joint is really the foot. The bones of the foot have elongated and fused together to form a single bone, which ends in four toes.

Amazing facts

- The killdeer (*Charadrius vociferus*) gets its name from its piercing call, which sounds like 'kill-dee, kill-dee'.
- The jacana, or lily trotter, lives on ponds and lakes. It can swim, but it usually trots across the pond using lilypads as stepping stones.

▲ The jacana has very long toes, which spread its weight, allowing it to walk across floating leaves in ponds and lakes.

◄ Knots are wading birds with a straight probing beak for feeding on **invertebrates** that are found in mud.

Parrots

The order Psittaciformes contains the brightly coloured parrots, parakeets, cockatoos, budgerigars and macaws. Parrots are found in Australasia, South America and Central America, as well as in India, South-east Asia, West Africa and North Africa.

Features

This order is made up of two families: cockatoos (Cacatuidae) and parrots (Psittacidae). The term parrot can be used to indicate either the Psittacidae alone or the entire order. Cockatoos have a head crest and are usually less colourful than parrots.

Most parrots have a large head with a short neck, and a thick, hooked beak with a fleshy tongue. Their feet are large and strong, with two toes pointing forwards and two backwards to give them a good grip. This allows them to climb trees and pick up food. They spend most of the day in the highest branches of trees, flying off only to find food. Their wings are narrow and pointed, allowing them to fly easily between trees.

Amazing facts

- Grey parrots are expert at copying human speech. Some have been taught more than 750 words.

- The bat parrot hangs upside down from tree branches.

- About 10 per cent of parrot species, including the hooded parrot and grey-cheeked parrot, dig into termite mounds to hollow out a nesting chamber for themselves. The termites attack them at first, but become used to the presence of the bird.

◀ The sulphur-crested cockatoo has a yellow crest and yellow undersides to its wings.

Food

Parrots typically feed on fruit, nuts and seeds, using their beak like a nutcracker to break open tough food. The brightly coloured lorikeets (*Trichoglossus* **species**) feed mainly on nectar and pollen. Their tongues have a brush-like tip to help them lap up nectar. The flightless kakapo of New Zealand searches for leaves, young shoots, berries and moss on the forest floor.

Nesting sites

Parrots are sociable birds and they tend to live in pairs or in flocks. They are noisy birds, too, calling to each other as they fly along. Most parrots nest in holes in trees. The female lays between two and eight white eggs. The young are born naked and helpless. They are fed with partially digested food that is **regurgitated** to them by the parents.

▲ Macaws are brightly coloured parrots that come from South America. Many are found in **tropical** rainforests.

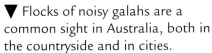

▼ Flocks of noisy galahs are a common sight in Australia, both in the countryside and in cities.

Classification key

CLASS	Aves
ORDER	**Psittaciformes**
FAMILIES	2 – Cacatuidae (cockatoos) and Psittacidae (parrots)
SPECIES	about 340

Kingfishers

The order Coraciiformes is made up of ten families including kingfishers, hornbills, bee-eaters, kookaburras, rollers and motmots. These birds are found around the world in a variety of habitats including rivers and lakes, grassland and woodland.

Kingfishers and their relatives are stocky birds with big heads and small feet. Most have brightly coloured feathers. All **species** have the three front toes joined for at least part of their length. Their wings are generally broad, but the bee-eater has long, pointed wings allowing it to perform aerial acrobatics as it catches bees. Hornbills are named after their large beak with a casque, the helmet-shaped armour that lies on top of its beak. To support the weight of its massive beak, the top two bones in the spine are fused together.

Feeding

Most of these birds are **carnivores**, feeding on fish, small **mammals** and **reptiles**, insects and spiders, although hornbills eat fruit, too. The shape of the beak reflects their carnivorous diet – it is relatively heavy to enable the bird to deal with **prey**. Kingfishers hunt along rivers by sitting perfectly still on a perch and waiting for fish to swim close to the surface. The bird then dives down, head first, into the water and grabs the fish with its spear-like beak. It flies back to its perch where it beats the fish against the perch to kill it.

▲ This Eurasian kingfisher is diving head-first into the water to catch a fish.

Classification key	
CLASS	Aves
ORDER	**Coraciiformes**
FAMILIES	10
SPECIES	more than 200

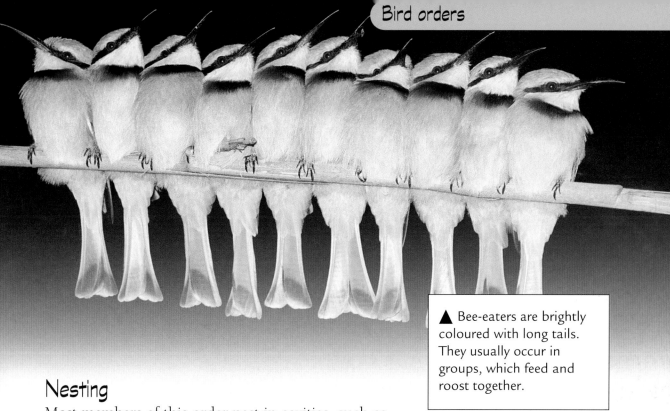

▲ Bee-eaters are brightly coloured with long tails. They usually occur in groups, which feed and roost together.

Nesting

Most members of this order nest in cavities, such as burrows in the riverbank or hollows of trees. Most hornbills build their nests in tree hollows, although some live on the ground. With the female inside, the entrance is sealed with mud, leaving a tiny slit through which the male can pass food to the female. The great Indian hornbill stays inside her nest for three months. She breaks out when her single egg has hatched, and her chick reseals the hole and stays inside for another month, until it is ready to leave the nest.

▲ The ground hornbill is the largest of the hornbills. It has black feathers and patches of red skin on its face and throat.

Amazing facts

- Hoopoes' nests stink due to accumulation of droppings and old food. This is thought to put off **predators**!
- The yellow-billed hornbill often hunts with dwarf mongooses. The mongooses disturb locusts, which the birds like to hunt. In return the hornbill warns the mongooses of approaching predators.
- The European bee-eater preys on bees and other stinging insects. When a bee is caught, the bee-eater squashes the insect's body in its beak to expel the poison, making it safe to eat.

Woodpeckers and toucans

Woodpeckers and toucans have thick bones in their skull,
a heavy beak and clawed feet that allow them to climb trees.
Woodpeckers are found all over the world, except in Madagascar
and Australia. Toucans are found in Central and South America.

Hammering wood

The woodpecker is named after the way it hammers the tree
trunk with its beak. It does this to dig out a hole for its nest and
to find food. The beak is hard and sharp, and it is used like a
chisel. Powerful muscles in the neck drive the head forwards and
backwards for hours. The skull is thick and covered by muscles,
which protect the head and cushion the impact of the beak
hammering against the trunk. The nostrils have an overlay of
fine feathers to stop dust entering the lungs. Woodpeckers are
climbers and they have four toes arranged with two pointing
forwards and two pointing backwards. Each toe ends in a sharp
claw for gripping the trunk. The tail feathers are stiff and they are
pushed against the tree to lend more support when the bird is
vertical, a bit like a third leg.

Although woodpeckers can sing, they tend to
rely on drumming as a means of communicating.
They knock their beak against a hollow trunk to
produce a drumming sound that carries
through woodland.

▼ The bright yellow beak of
the toco toucan is the size of a
banana, but it is not as heavy
as it looks because the beak
contains lots of air spaces.

Food

Woodpeckers feed on beetles, adult insects and insect **larvae** that they find in tree trunks. The birds have long tongues, which enable them to reach into insect tunnels to pull out a meal. The tongue is covered in sticky **saliva** and it also has **barbs** that grip the **prey**. Some woodpeckers, such as flickers, forage on the ground for ants.

The toucan feeds mostly on fruit, although some will eat insects. It uses its pincer-like beak to grip fruit and rip it into smaller pieces.

Nest holes

Woodpeckers and toucans nest in holes, either in holes they have made themselves in trees or holes that already exist in dead trees or even burrows in the ground. Once they have made their nest hole, they will defend it against other birds that try to steal it.

▲ The great spotted woodpecker (*Dendrocopos major*) is easily identified by its black and white feathers and bright red spot on its underside.

Classification key

CLASS	Aves
ORDER	**Piciformes**
FAMILIES	6
SPECIES	more than 400

Amazing facts

○ In 1995 the launch of the space shuttle *Discovery* was delayed after a pair of flickers (a type of woodpecker) had pecked holes in the foam **insulation** of the shuttles' external fuel tank.

○ Toucan chicks grow slowly. More than a month passes before their feathers start to grow and they do not leave the nest hole until they are about two months old.

▼ The aracari is the only toucan that roosts in holes overnight.

Perching birds

There are more than 5700 **species** of perching birds, or passerines. They are found in a variety of habitats around the world, but most commonly in woodlands, shrubs and gardens.

One feature that distinguishes these birds from other orders is the foot. A perching bird has four toes that can grip branches, enabling it to perch. There are three forward-pointing toes and one that points backwards. The hind toe is large, strong and well developed. When a perching bird lands on a branch, the flexing of its legs forces the **tendons** in its legs to tighten. This causes the slender toes to curl tightly around the branch.

Songbirds

All passerines are able to sing. Most birds can make sounds, but not all can sing. A bird's syrinx (voice box) is located at the bottom of the windpipe. The syrinx is made up of a number of membranes and it is the vibration of these membranes that creates a sound. Muscles around the syrinx change the shape of the membranes, which in turn changes the sound. The more muscles, the more varied the sounds that can be produced, and songbirds have more of these muscles than other birds.

Classification key	
CLASS	Aves
ORDER	**Passeriformes**
SUB-ORDERS	Tyranni and Passeres
FAMILIES	60
SPECIES	about 5700

▼ Crows eat whatever they can find on the ground, including eggs, chicks, insects, fruits, seeds and small rodents.

Each species has its own distinctive song and a particular time at which it sings. Songbirds sing for many reasons – a male may sing to warn other males to stay away or to attract a female. Some males and females sing duets. Singing is often triggered by light, with most birds singing at dawn, although a few sing at night. More singing takes place in the **breeding** season.

Two sub-orders

This large order is divided into two sub-orders: Tyranni and Passeres. The two sub-orders are distinguished by the number of muscles in the syrinx or voice box. Tyranni have between one and four pairs of muscles, while members of Passeres have between five and nine pairs, giving them a greater range of songs. Birds classified within the sub-order Tyranni include the more primitive perching birds, such as woodcreepers, antbirds, bellbirds and lyrebirds. The sub-order Passeres is made up of songbirds such as nightingales, thrushes, finches and warblers.

▶ The Northern Cardinal is a red bird from the eastern USA. These birds are strongly **territorial** and have a loud, whistling song.

Amazing facts

● Perching birds continue to grip the branch even when they are asleep, so they do not fall off!

● A red-eyed vireo (*Vireo olivaceus*) from the USA is known to have sung more than 22,000 songs in one day.

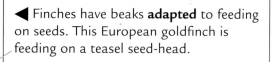

◀ Finches have beaks **adapted** to feeding on seeds. This European goldfinch is feeding on a teasel seed-head.

▲ A male weaver bird builds its complex nest, with an entrance on the underside, out of reach of predators.

Perching bird nests

The most common form of nest is a cup-shaped nest made of twigs, moss, grass and leaves, held in the fork of a tree or shrub. These nests are often hidden as they blend well with their surroundings. About a quarter of perching bird **species** build nests with domes or nest in small holes in trees.

Swallows and martins build cup-shaped mud nests. They collect mud from puddles and pools and mix it with **saliva**. Using their beaks, they form the mud into a cup-shaped nest that is attached to walls under eaves or in buildings. The nest is built up in layers, with the new bits of mud being left to dry before more is added.

Weaving nests

Some perching birds weave their elaborate nests, for example orioles, oropendolas and weaver birds. These birds have a beak that acts like a needle, which they use to thread thin strips of leaf under and over other threads. The female oropendola rips off a long strip of leaf and secures one end around a twig. She bends the strip into a hoop to form the entrance to the nest. She uses more strips to weave the walls, gradually building a nest up to 1.5 metres long, all the time working from the inside.

Amazing facts

- The sociable weavers of southern Africa nest in **colonies** of up to 300 birds. The large, interconnecting nest, made from dry grass, forms a huge woven mass around the branches of a single tree.

- Fieldfares (*Turdus pilaris*) scream a warning if a magpie approaches. This summons other fieldfares who will dive bomb the magpie until it goes away.

Caring for young

The chicks of perching birds are completely helpless. They need to be fed by their parents until they are fully **fledged** and can look after themselves. The chicks demand food all the time and parent birds may bring food to the nest hundreds of times each day. Not only do they have to feed their young, but they must protect them from **predators** such as magpies, hawks or snakes. The parent birds have to continue to care for their chicks until the chicks start to grow their proper feathers and are ready to fly. The nest by this time will have become very overcrowded. Most chicks will continue to be fed by their parents for some time after fledging.

▲ Most perching birds build a cup-shaped nest using materials found near by, such as twigs, leaves, moss and feathers.

◀ This reed warbler is feeding a cuckoo chick. A cuckoo replaced one of the warbler's eggs with one of her own. The warbler will raise the cuckoo as her own.

47

The song thrush

The song thrush is a well-known garden and woodland songbird with a spotted chest. It is found in Europe, North Africa, north-west Asia, Australia and New Zealand. The song thrush has a distinctive song, which it sings at dusk.

Raising chicks

The **breeding** season in the northern **temperate** zone is long and lasts from March to August. During this time a pair of thrushes may have two or three broods. The female builds her nest in trees and shrubs. It is formed from twigs, grass and moss, cemented together and thickly lined with mud, dung and rotten wood, often mixed with leaves. It can take three weeks to complete.

The female lays between three and five eggs, which she **incubates** for about fifteen days. The chicks are fed mostly on worms, but adult song thrushes will also eat slugs, caterpillars and even fruit. They like to eat snails, which they break into by smashing against a stone.

The chicks are ready to **fledge** at about fourteen days, but if the nest is disturbed, they can leave as early as nine days old. They creep and flutter from the nest, and remain in nearby shrubs for a few days.

Classification key

CLASS	Aves
ORDER	Passeriformes
FAMILY	Turdidae
GENUS	*Turdus*
SPECIES	***Turdus philomelos***

▲ A song thrush smashes snails against a rock with a flick of its head.

◄ The song thrush usually sings from a tree-top perch at dusk and dawn, repeating phrases of its song three or four times.

The chicks are more or less flightless at first, but within a week they can fly well. They continue to be fed by their parents while they are learning to find food themselves. The young birds will be independent about three weeks after leaving the nest. Many of the fledglings will die over the winter, and only one in every five fledglings will survive until the following spring. Many of the adults die, too, with only three in every five surviving over winter.

Under threat

The numbers of song thrushes are declining, and the song thrush is categorized as a bird of serious conservation concern. The decline is caused by a lack of food and nesting sites. This has been triggered by changes in farming methods, such as the removal of hedgerows and the use of pesticides on crops. Farmers can improve the habitat for song thrushes by allowing hedgerows to grow tall and thick, and by planting new areas of woodland on farmland.

Amazing fact

- Song thrushes are relatively short-lived birds, living an average of three or four years. A few can reach quite an advanced age. The oldest known wild song thrush was thirteen years old.

◄ Song thrush chicks are fed on earthworms and insect **larvae**. About half die during their first year.

Minor orders

Many of the orders within the class of Aves are small. They contain just a few families. Some contain just one family and a handful of **species**.

Order Phoenicopteriformes

Flamingos are large, long-legged wading birds with peculiar 'bent' bills through which they filter tiny **organisms** from the water. Flamingos fly with their legs and necks extended. They are highly social birds that come together in large groups to feed and **breed**. Most have white or pink **plumage**.

Classification key

CLASS	Aves
ORDER	**Phoenicopteriformes**
FAMILIES	1
SPECIES	5

Order Procellariiformes

The albatrosses south of the **equator**, shearwaters and petrels are seabirds of the open oceans. They spend their lives gliding over the ocean, feeding on fish and squid. They only come on to land to breed. The largest albatrosses have a 4-metre wingspan. Their three front toes are webbed. All the birds in this order lay a single white egg, which they **incubate** for about ten weeks, and their chicks take several months to develop. These birds are also known as tube-noses, named after the paired tubular nostrils on top of the beak. They have well-developed salt glands that enable them to drink salt water. The salt gland filters excess salt from the blood and removes it through these external nostrils.

Classification key

CLASS	Aves
ORDER	**Procellariiformes**
FAMILIES	4
SPECIES	100

▼ The wandering albatross weighs 8 kilograms and has a wingspan of 3.5 metres.

▲ The pink colour of the flamingo comes from a substance in the food that it eats.

Order Pelecaniformes

Pelecaniformes is a large group of sea birds. The order includes pelicans, cormorants, gannets, tropic birds, frigate birds, anhingas and boobies. They are the only birds to have all four toes webbed to give them an extra push in the water. They are generally large birds with long wings and short legs. Most have a pouch of bare skin between the bones of the lower jaw, but it is most developed in the pelican. When pelicans dive into the sea, the pouch balloons out to form a net that traps fish.

Boobies and gannets plunge straight into the water from heights of 30 metres or more to catch fish, using sharp beaks with serrated edges to hold their slippery **prey**. Anhingas are unusual as they swim with only their head and neck above water. The neck is kinked to form a Z-shape, which allows the bird to straighten its neck with great speed and spear fish in the water. Frigate birds spend their lives gliding over the oceans. They come down to the surface to catch fish, although they often obtain food by stealing from other birds.

▲ The pelican has a large throat pouch to scoop fish from the water.

Classification key

CLASS	Aves
ORDER	**Pelecaniformes**
FAMILIES	6
SPECIES	67

51

Order Ciconiiformes

This order includes birds such as herons, storks and egrets. They are generally large **aquatic** birds with broad, rounded wings and long legs, which are ideal for wading in shallow water. However, their toes are not webbed. These **carnivorous** birds feed on frogs and fish. Most members of this order live in **colonies**. In some classifications the vultures of North and South America are placed in this order. However, DNA evidence suggests that they should be classified with the birds of **prey**.

Classification key	
CLASS	Aves
ORDER	**Ciconiiformes**
FAMILIES	6
SPECIES	120

▼ Herons have long, straight beaks, which they use to spear fish.

Order Columbiformes

Pigeons and doves are found around the world with the exception of the polar regions. They are plump birds with small heads, a short beak and short toes. They all have a large **crop**, which is the source of 'pigeon milk' that is fed to the young. However, this milk is very different to that produced by female **mammals**. The adult birds eat mainly fruits and seeds. These birds are related to the dodo, a large, flightless bird that was hunted to **extinction** 200 years ago.

Classification key	
CLASS	Aves
ORDER	**Columbiformes**
FAMILY	1
SPECIES	more than 300

◄ The rock dove, or pigeon, is found in towns and cities across the world.

Order Cuculiformes

Cuckoos and roadrunners are large, land-living birds with long, often downward-curved beaks and long tails. Their feet have two toes pointing forwards and two pointing backwards. Cuckoos eat mostly insects, while roadrunners eat rattlesnakes.

Classification key

CLASS	Aves
ORDER	**Cuculiformes**
FAMILIES	uncertain
SPECIES	143

Order Apodiformes

Hummingbirds and swifts have short, stout wings. They have long flight feathers – an **adaptation** to their fast, hovering flight. These birds have short legs that end in extremely small, weak feet. Hummingbirds have a long, slender bill with a long tongue adapted for nectar feeding. They frequently have bright, shiny **plumage**. Swifts have a short bill with a wide mouth. They have a short tongue and catch insects in mid-air.

Classification key

CLASS	Aves
ORDER	**Apodiformes**
FAMILIES	3
SPECIES	more than 400

▶ Hummingbirds dart from flower to flower in search of energy-rich nectar.

The remaining orders are not described in detail in this book. Their classification is given in the table below.

Order	Example	Families	Species
CAPRIMULGIFORMES	Nighthawks, nightjars and frogmouths	5	113
COLIIFORMES	Mousebirds	1	5
GAVIIFORMES	Loons and divers	1	5
GRUIFORMES	Rails and cranes	11	110
MUSOPHAGIFORMES	Turacos	1	23
PODICIPEDIFORMES	Grebes	1	21
TROGONIFORMES	Trogons	1	39

Birds under threat

Just over 200 years ago, sailors killed the last remaining dodos on the island of Mauritius. The dodo was a large, flightless bird that lived in forests. Since that time a number of birds have become **extinct**, including the passenger pigeon and the great auk. Today, many **species** of birds are under threat of extinction.

Habitat change

Around the world, habitats, such as woodland and grassland, are being cleared to make way for new towns, roads and industry. **Tropical** forests are home to thousands of species of birds, but this habitat is being lost rapidly. Wetlands, such as salt marshes, are being drained and used for new farmland, and estuaries are being developed into docks and marinas.

Amazing facts

- Of the 140 native species of birds present on the Hawaiian Islands before the arrival of people, 69 are now extinct, 30 are listed as endangered and 15 are on the brink of extinction.
- The New Zealand kakapo is a flightless parrot. It is one of the most endangered parrots in the world with a population of less than 100 birds.

▼ Tropical rainforests are home to thousands of species of birds, but each year more of the forest is cleared or burnt to make way for buildings or farmland.

Many birds are found on farmland where there is a mosaic of habitats such as hedgerows, woodland and grassland. As farming methods have become more intensive, farmers have ripped up hedgerows to create larger fields and they spray their crops with pesticides and weedkillers. Birds may eat seed contaminated with chemicals. Pesticides, such as DDT, killed millions of birds during the 1960s, with birds of **prey** being the most affected. DDT is now banned in most parts of the world. Birds are often at the top of a food chain as they eat smaller animals such as insects. If anything happens to the animals lower down the chain, the birds that eat them are affected, too.

▲ This barn owl may have been poisoned by eating prey animals contaminated with pesticides.

Island birds

Many endangered species of birds live on islands where they may not have had any natural **predators**. Then people arrived from other parts of the world, bringing dogs, cats and rats with them, too. These animals preyed on native birds, such as the kiwi, kea and kakapo of New Zealand, and caused their numbers to decline.

Pet trade

Birds are popular pets, especially the more colourful birds such as parrots, cockatoos and budgerigars. Often these birds are collected from the wild, transported across the world and sold in pet shops. For every bird on sale in a pet shop, many more will have died on the journey.

◀ These birds were probably caught in the wild. Many die when they are caught and transported to market.

Protecting birds

One of the best ways of protecting a bird is to protect its habitat. A bird relies on its habitat for food and nesting places, so if its habitat disappears or is changed, the bird will not survive. By protecting the whole habitat, all the plants and animals that live there can thrive.

◀ The nene breeds very well in captivity and now there are thousands of these geese.

Captive breeding

Sometimes a bird's habitat may have completely disappeared or there are so few individuals surviving that the bird can only be saved by keeping it in a zoo or wildlife park. Birds such as the Hawaiian goose, or nene, and the Californian condor have been saved from **extinction** in this way. Individuals were caught in the wild and kept in zoos to **breed** and slowly increase in number. The captive breeding scheme of the nene at the Wildfowl and Wetland Trust at Slimbridge, in the UK, has been so successful that the nene has been reintroduced to protected areas in Hawaii.

▲ Research projects on the hyacinth macaw are producing valuable information that will help the conservation of this parrot.

Amazing facts

- The Portland General Electric Power company in Oregon, USA, builds 3-metre-high extensions to its telegraph poles to provide safe nest sites for ospreys, well away from the lethal power lines.

- In 1987 the last Californian condors (*Gymnogyps californianus*) were removed from the wild and placed in captivity where they have bred well. By the end of 1998 the population consisted of 146 individuals. Some condors were released back into the wild, and in 2001 the first egg for 15 years was laid in the wild.

CITES

CITES (the Convention on International Trade in Endangered **Species** of Wild Fauna and Flora) is an international agreement between governments. Its aim is to ensure that international trade in specimens of wild animals and plants does not threaten their survival. Today, CITES gives protection to more than 30,000 species of animal and plant. Just under 1700 species of birds are given protection. There are three levels of protection, and 146 bird species, which are considered at the greatest risk of extinction, have been awarded the highest level of protection. These are mostly species of parrots, birds of **prey**, game birds and cranes.

▶ Captive breeding has enabled the Californian condor to survive.

Classification

Scientists have found and classified about 2 million different types of animals. With so many **species** it is important that they are classified into groups. The groups show how living **organisms** are related by **evolution** and where they belong in the natural world. A scientist identifies an animal by looking at its features, for example, by counting the number of legs or what teeth it has. Animals that share the same features belong to the same species. Species with similar characteristics are placed in the same genus. The genera are grouped together in families, families are grouped into orders and orders are grouped into classes. Classes are grouped together in phyla (singular: phylum) and finally, phyla are grouped into kingdoms. Kingdoms are the largest groups and are at the highest level. There are five kingdoms: monerans (bacteria), protists (single-celled organisms), fungi, plants and animals.

Naming an animal

Each species has a unique scientific name, usually called its Latin name, consisting of two words. The first word is the name of the genus to which the organism belongs and the second is the name of its species. For example, the Latin name of the mute swan is *Cygnus olor* and that of the black swan is *Cygnus atratus*. This tells us that these animals are grouped in the same genus but are different species. Latin names are used to avoid confusion. For example, there are many 'robins' around the world. The European robin is *Erithacus rubecula* while the American robin is *Turdus migratorius*. The bird *Gavia arctica* is called the black-throated diver in the UK and the Arctic loon in the USA. Sometimes there are very small differences between individuals that belong to the same species. So, there is an extra division called a sub-species. To show that an animal belongs to a sub-species, another name is added to the end of the Latin name. For example, the military macaw of Mexico is *Ara militaris mexicana*, while the one that is found in Bolivia is called *Ara militaris boliviana*.

◄ There are many species of crane. This is the grey crowned crane, *Balearica regulorum,* from East and South Africa.

This table shows how a bald eagle is classified.

Classification	Example: bald eagle	Features
Kingdom	Animalia	Bald eagles belong to the kingdom Animalia because they have many cells, need to eat food and are formed from a **fertilized** egg.
Phylum	Chordata	An animal from the phylum Chordata has a strengthening rod called a notochord running down its back.
Sub-phylum	Vertebrata	Animals that have a backbone, a series of small bones running down the back enclosing the spinal cord, are called vertebrates. The backbone replaces the notochord.
Class	Aves	Class Aves is birds. It includes animals with bodies covered in feathers and front limbs modified to form wings.
Order	Falconiformes	The birds of **prey** have a powerful, hooked beak and strong, muscular feet with long, sharp claws.
Family	Accipitridae	Members of the family Accipitridae are active **predators** and build nests made of sticks. The insides of their eggs are green-tinted.
Genus	*Haliaeetus*	A genus is a group of species that are more closely related to one another than to any other group in the family. *Haliaeetus* refers to the genus.
Species	*leucocephalus*	A species is a grouping of individuals that **interbreed** successfully. The full bald eagle species name is *Haliaeetus leucocephalus*.

Bird evolution

The **evolution** of birds goes back to the time of the dinosaurs, about 200 million years ago. It is most likely that birds **evolved** from a group of dinosaurs called coelurosaurians. They were small, **carnivorous** animals with long necks. No one is sure what happened next as there is no fossil evidence. Some believe that tree-living dinosaurs gradually developed flight as they glided from tree to tree. Others believe that birds rose from ground-dwelling dinosaurs that could run and leap.

Archaeopteryx was the first known bird with feathers and it dates back 150 million years. It is considered to be the missing link between **reptiles** and birds. It was an animal the size of a chicken with feathers and wings. However, it also had reptile features such as teeth. The first bird known to have developed wings that could sustain flight was *Ichthyornis*, which lived 80 million years ago. It had teeth and probably ate fish. About 65 million years ago the remaining dinosaurs became **extinct**, but the birds survived. They became very common and **adapted** themselves to many different habitats. By about 40 million years ago, all the modern groups of birds were present.

▲ Kingfishers first appeared more than 40 million years ago.

▼ This *Archaeopteryx* is one of the most important fossils in bird evolution, as it is considered to be the first animal with feathers.

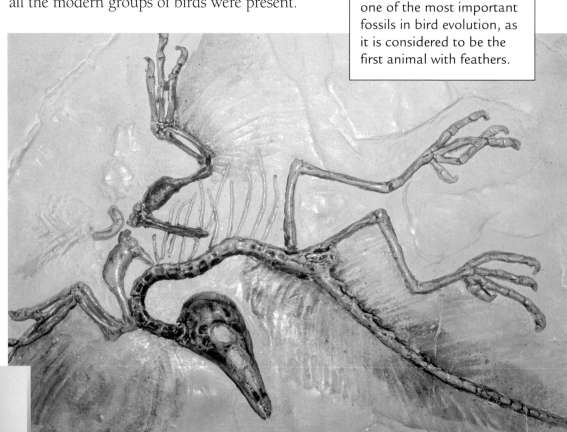

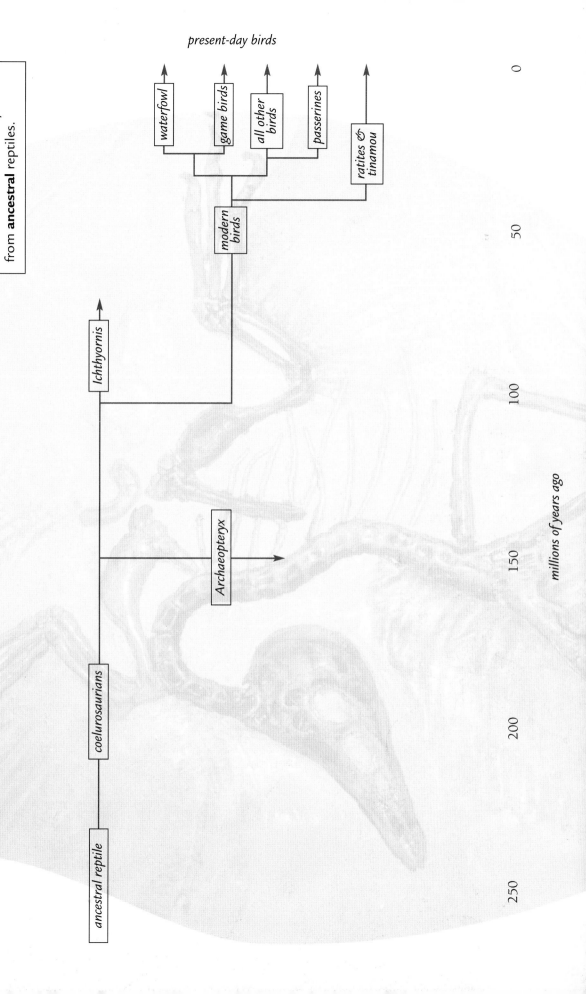

▶ This diagram shows the evolution of modern-day birds from **ancestral** reptiles.

present-day birds

waterfowl

game birds

all other birds

passerines

ratites & tinamou

modern birds

Ichthyornis

Archaeopteryx

coelurosaurians

ancestral reptile

millions of years ago

0

50

100

150

200

250

Glossary

adapt change in order to cope with the environment

albumen white of an egg, made of protein and water

ancestor an individual from which an animal is descended

aquatic living in water

barb small hook

blubber thick layer of fat under the skin that helps animals keep warm

breed mate and produce young

buoyant able to float

carnivore animal that eats other animals

carrion dead or decaying animals

clutch set of eggs laid by one bird and incubated at the same time

colony large group of animals

crop pouch off the oesophagus (a tube running from the mouth to the stomach) in which food can be stored

egg tooth sharp tip on the beak of a chick used by the chick to hatch out of the egg

embryo unborn chick at a very early stage of development in the egg

endothermic having a body temperature that is kept constant regardless of the temperature of the surroundings, often referred to as warm blooded

equator imaginary line that runs around the centre of the Earth

evolution slow process of change in living organisms to make them better able to adapt to their environment

evolve to change very slowly over a long period of time

extinct no longer in existence, permanently disappeared

fertilize cause a female to produce young (an egg or live young) through the introduction of male reproductive material

fledge leave the nest, learn to fly

gizzard pouch of a bird's stomach that is full of grit and helps to grind up food

heat exchanger arrangement of blood vessels that allows the transfer of heat from one to the other

incubate keep eggs at the right temperature for the development of the chicks, either by the parent bird sitting on them or by covering them with leaves or earth

insulate keep warm, for example feathers and blubber keep birds warm

interbreed mate with another animal of the same species

invertebrate animal that does not have a backbone

keel ridge or extension along the breastbone of a bird that allows the attachment of flight muscles

larva (plural: **larvae**) young animal that looks different from the adult and which changes shape as it develops

mammal class of vertebrates that feed their young milk, are usually covered in hair and have a constant body temperature

mate (noun) reproduction partner of the opposite sex

mate (verb) ability of male to fertilize the eggs of a female of the same species

migrate regular journey made by an animal, often linked to the changes of the seasons

moult annual shedding of feathers, followed by the growth of a new set

nictitating membrane thin membrane that moves sideways across the eye, also called the third eyelid

nidicolous newly hatched bird that is blind, naked and completely helpless for the first weeks of its life

nidifugous newly hatched chick with a covering of downy feathers and open eyes, which can run around and feed within minutes of hatching

organism living being such as an animal, plant or bacterium

plumage birds' feathers

predator animal that hunts another animal

preening cleaning the feathers

prey animal that is hunted by another animal

raptor another name for a bird of prey

regurgitate bring the contents of the stomach back into the mouth

reptile ectothermic (having a body temperature that changes with the surrounding temperature), egg-laying vertebrate with tough skin covered in scales

saliva fluid produced in the mouth to help chew and digest food

skeleton bony framework of an animal

species group of individuals that share many characteristics and which can interbreed to produce offspring

streamlined having a slim shape that moves through air or water easily

temperate relating to regions of the Earth which lie between the tropics and the poles, with mild climates

tendon strong band, made of protein, that joins a muscle to a bone

territory range or area claimed by an animal or group of animals

thermals warm air currents that enable some birds to glide effortlessly

torpid/torpor inactive, a state of inactivity

tropical relating to the hot regions of the world between the tropic of Cancer and the tropic of Capricorn

tropics hot regions of the world between the tropic of Cancer and the tropic of Capricorn

vertebrate animal that has a backbone

Further information

BOOKS TO READ

Attenborough, David, *Life of Birds* (BBC Books, 1998). This book covers the great variety of birds, their life cycle, feeding, behaviour and much more.

Grove, Noel, *Birds of North America* (Hugh Lauter Levin Associates, 1996). This book introduces the reader to six groups of birds found in North America, songbirds, raptors, game birds, specialists, shorebirds and waterbirds. Illustrated with 200 colour photographs.

Hume, Rob, *RSPB Complete Birds of Britain and Europe* (Dorling Kindersley, 2002). Photographic guidebook to the identification of birds found in Britain and Europe, together with introductory information on the biology of birds.

USEFUL WEBSITES

http://www.rspb.org.uk
Website of the Royal Society for the Protection of Birds (RSPB), the leading ornithological society in Britain, with plenty of information on birds, their habitats and some of the threats to birds.

http://museum.nhm.uga.edu/gawildlife/birds/birds.html
Website covering all forms of animal life including birds. All the orders of birds are considered together with lists of specific birds found in the state of Georgia.

http://www.nhm.org/birds/
Website of the Natural History Museum of Los Angeles County Foundation, which provides general information about bird evolution and diversity, anatomy and physiology, adaptations and behaviour, flight mechanics and conservation.

Disclaimer
All the Internet addresses (URLs) given in this book were valid at the time of going to press. However, due to the dynamic nature of the Internet, some addresses may have changed, or sites may have changed or ceased to exist since publication. While the author, the packager and Publishers regret any inconvenience this may cause readers, no responsibility for any such changes can be accepted by either the author, the packager or the Publishers.

Index

Titles in the *Animal Kingdom* series include:

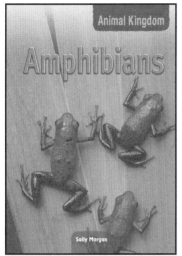

Hardback   1 844 43773 6

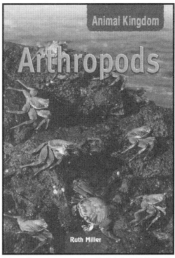

Hardback   1 844 43772 8

Hardback   1 844 43771 X

Hardback   1 844 43767 1

Hardback   1 844 43766 3

Hardback   1 844 43769 8

Hardback   1 844 43768 X

Hardback   1 844 43774 4

Find out about the other titles in this series on our website www.raintreepublishers.co.uk